100 GREATEST MOMENTS in IRISH HISTORY

Written by Tara Gallagher

Illustrated by Hannah Bailey

Designed by Alyssa Peacock

Gill & Macmillan

Gill & Macmillan
Hume Avenue, Park West, Dublin 12
with associated companies throughout the world

www.gillmacmillan.ie

Copyright © 2011, Teapot Press Ltd
ISBN 9780717149704
Produced by Teapot Press Ltd

Printed in the EU

A CIP catalogue record for this book
is available from the British Library.

5 4 3 2 1

Contents

33 1689
The Siege of Derry

34 1 July 1690
The Battle of the Boyne

35 1691
Battle of Aughrim

36 1695-1728
The Penal Laws

37 1713-1726
Jonathan Swift writes *Gulliver's Travels*

38 1739-1741
Famine

39 13 Apr 1742
World premiere of Handel's Messiah in Dublin

40 1759
Foundation of Guinness

41 1779
First parade of Volunteers in Dublin

42 1795
Foundation of Orange Order

43 1798
Rebellion in Wexford, Antrim and Down

44 1798
French force lands in Mayo and Donegal

45 1801
Act of Union

46 23 July 1803
Robert Emmet's Rising

47 15 Aug 1808
Foundation of the Christian Brothers

48 1829
Daniel O'Connell becomes known as 'Liberator of the Nation'

49 1 Sept 1831
Dublin Zoo opens

50 1845-1846
The Great Famine

51 11 Sept 1855
Ireland's first ever cricket international

52 1858
Irish Republican Brotherhood formed

53 29 March 1859
First copy of the *Irish Times* printed

54 1867
Rise of Fenians and the Manchester Martyrs

55 1870
The Home Rule Association set up by Isaac Butt

56 1872
First Dublin trams put into service

57 21 Oct 1879
The Irish National Land League founded

58 1881
Land Act

59 1 Nov 1884
Gaelic Athletic formed by Michael Cusack

60 July 1893
Gaelic League founded by Douglas Hyde

61 14 Feb 1895
First performance of *The Importance of Being Earnest*

62 1897
Bram Stoker's *Dracula* published

63 1905
Sinn Féin founded

64 20 Dec 1909
The Volta, Ireland's first cinema, opens

65 15 April 1912
Titanic sinks after hitting iceberg

66 1913
The Dublin Lockout

67 1913
Irish Citizen Army set up

68 8 Aug 1914
Shackleton's *Endurance* sets sail for Antarctica

69 April 1916
Easter Rising

70 1919
Irish Volunteers and Citizen Army merge to form IRA

71 1919
The first Dáil meets

72 1919
War of Independence

73 1920
Act for partition of Ireland passed

74 1921
Anglo-Irish Treaty signed

75 22 Aug 1922
Michael Collins dies

76 1922
Irish Free State established

77 April 1923
Sean O'Casey's first play opens

78 14 Nov 1923
WB Yeats wins the Nobel Literature Prize

79 1932
Eamon de Valera in power

80 20 May 1932
Amelia Earhart lands at Culmore, Co. Derry

81 1937
Constitution of Ireland

82 1939
Outbreak of World War II – the Emergency

83 31 Jan 1953
The car ferry Princess Victoria sinks in gales in the Irish Sea

84 31 Dec 1961
RTÉ begins broadcasting

85 1968
Start of NI Troubles

86 21 Mar 1970
Dana is first Irish winner of Eurovision

87 1972
Bloody Sunday

88 1 Jan 1973
Ireland joins EEC

89 1979
Pope John Paul II visits Ireland

90 March 1987
National Lottery launched in Ireland

91 26 July 1987
Stephen Roche wins Tour de France

92 1990
Mary Robinson first female President of Ireland

93 30 Apr 1994
Riverdance first performed

94 1995
Seamus Heaney – Nobel Prize winner

95 1998
Good Friday Agreement

96 15 Aug 1998
Omagh bombing

97 2002
Currency changes from punt to euro

98 Dec 2004
Robbery of Belfast's Northern Bank

99 2007
New Northern Ireland Assembly meets for the first time

100 2009
Ireland's rugby team wins the Grand Slam and Triple Crown in the Six Nations

1

7,000-6,500 BC First settlements built at Mount Sandel

Stone age people hunted animals both for food and for their pelts.

Mount Sandel lies on high ground overlooking the River Bann in Co. Derry, and is the remains of a small collection of circular huts. It provides evidence of the first people who lived in what is now Ireland.

These Mesolitihic or Middle Stone Age people were hunter-gatherers, meaning instead of farming they gathered nuts, berries, and other plants, and hunted animals such as rabbits, birds, and wild boar with stone-tipped weapons.

2

3,500 BC Building of Newgrange

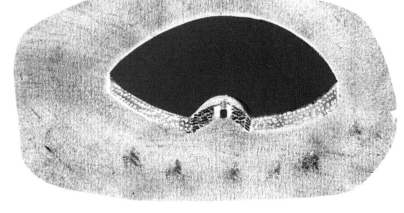

As New Stone Age people could not work metal, Newgrange was built using only tools made of stone and wood.

The Neolithic , or New Stone Age people left extraordinary monuments: great stone tombs for the dead covered by mounds of earth. The most spectacular is the passage tomb at Newgrange, Co. Meath. The tomb is exactly aligned so that every year on the shortest day of the year (21 December) the sun shines through a tiny opening at the entrance to light up the inner burial chamber.

③ 500 BC
Celts arrive in Ireland

Celtic warriors had bronze spears, swords, and shields. These were much more advanced than the older stone weapons.

Beginning around 500 BC, the Celts reached Ireland after conquering Western Europe, and settled in waves over the next few centuries. They spoke a language called Gaelic, and as well as being fierce warriors, also created beautiful artwork and poetry.

As there was no money, how rich your tribe was depended on how many cattle it had. The Chieftains or kings laid down the law, helped by the druids, who were similar to today's priests and judges, and the fili, who were the poets and storytellers.

④ AD 400
Christianity introduced by St Patrick

Born in Britain, at 16 years old Patrick was captured as a slave and spent six years as a shepherd in Ireland. Patrick became a priest, and later heard the voice of God again, telling him to return. Travelling around the island, he converted hundreds of people to Christianity.

St Patrick is said to have used the shamrock to explain the Holy Trinity to the Irish, thus giving them their national symbol.

⑤ 600-800
Age of Insular Art

After St Patrick brought Christianity to Ireland, monasteries became the biggest settlements throughout the island, creating centres of learning, religion, and especially art. Insular art was a type or style of art with intricate, geometric patterns that was produced in and around the monasteries of Ireland and Great Britain. Irish monasteries were famous throughout Europe for the ornate metalwork and beautifully illustrated books the monks created, the most famous example of which is the Book of Kells, named after the Abbey of Kells in Co. Meath where it was kept during the Middle Ages.

The Tara Brooch and the Ardagh Chalice both feature beautiful examples of filigree metalwork.

⑥ 795
Vikings begin to raid Ireland

Viking ships were designed to strike fear into the heart of the enemy with their boldly striped sails and dragon- or snake-headed prows.

In 795, the first Viking longboats landed on the shore of Rathlin, an island off the coast of Co. Antrim. A fierce and warlike band of Scandanavian warriors and sailors, Vikings had been raiding Northern Europe for decades, and were now targeting Ireland's monasteries for their famous wealth. The monastery on Rathlin was ransacked and burned, as were many more settlements and monasteries around Ireland in later years. Known as longboats, Viking ships rode high in the water, meaning that they could steer up rivers with shallow beds to raid settlements.

7

841 First Viking settlement of Dublin

By the 840s the Vikings had begun to build permanent bases in various strategic locations around Ireland where they could wait out the treacherous sailing conditons of winter. The settlements of Dublin, Cork, Limerick, and Waterford, all fortified harbours built on large rivers suitable for their longboats, grew to be the first Viking towns. Dublin was quickly established as a busy, crowded centre of trade and shipbuilding, with many ships

Viking dwellings were usually rectangular in shape, unlike the Celtic roundhouses.

being built at the docks on the banks of the River Liffey. The Vikings sailed all over Europe, bringing goods such as precious metals, leather, and cloth to trade with the native Irish and in towns.

The Vikings were traders, and established the towns of Dublin, Cork, Limerick, and Waterford.

8 1014 Battle of Clontarf and Brian Boru

Of all Ireland's warring factions, Brian Boru was the first king who could claim the title of High King of Ireland. Under Brian Boru's brother Mathgamain, their clan became the most powerful kingdom in Munster, and when Mathgamain was assassinated, Brian became king of Munster. Later, he allied with Máel Sechnaill, leader of the O'Neills, and with Ulster's powerful backing Brian crowned himself High King of Ireland in AD 1002. For 10 years Ireland was united under him, until in Leinster the Viking and Irish clans became unhappy with living under his rule. The King of Leinster, Máel Morda, joined with the king of the Dublin Vikings, Sitric Silkenbeard, and on Good Friday in 1014 they met Brian's armies on Clontarf beach. The Vikings had sent for help and had 1000 extra warriors, but as the battle raged on, the Munster forces slaughtered them. Of the Leinster-Viking army of 8000, it is said only one-quarter were left alive.

Brian Boru died after the battle, when a fleeing Viking warrior stumbled across his tent and killed him.

⑨ 1170 Strongbow sent to help the King of Leinster

Almost immediately after his men won Waterford back from the Vikings, Strongbow and Aoife were married in Waterford Cathedral.

Strongbow was a Norman knight loyal to King Henry II of England. When Diarmaid Mac Murchadha, the King of Leinster, asked for Strongbow's help in getting his throne back, Stongbow's Norman army helped him. Diarmaid gave his daughter Aoife's hand in marriage to Strongbow, then died, leaving him to be King of Leinster. Henry II then conquered Ireland with a large Norman army.

⑩ 1204 Building of Dublin Castle begins

In 1204, King John (Henry II's son) had a new castle built in Dublin to be the English seat of government in Ireland. The castle is built from limestone quarried from the Wicklow Mountains.

In earlier times, boats would have been able to sail from the moat right into the Liffey.

⑪ 1264 First Irish Parliament meets

A lot of land had been settled by the English Norman, or Anglo-Norman nobility, and by 1250, three-quarters of Ireland was controlled by them. On the 18 June 1264, the first recorded Irish Parliament was held in Castledermot, Co. Kildare, where the powerful landowners and nobles met to discuss the governing of their lands. The official Irish Parliament wasn't founded until 1297, and like the one before it represented only the Anglo-Irish ruling class.

12 1348
Bubonic plague hits Ireland

The bubonic plague, or 'Black Death' first hit Dublin in 1348. Spread by fleas that jumped from rats to bite humans, it killed one-third of the people in England, and probably the same in Ireland. The more crowded a place, the easier it was to catch. Builders of the largest and busiest towns in Ireland, the Normans were the worst hit.

The 'roses' in the song 'ring a ring o' roses' refer to the purple marks on the skin of the infected.

13 1366
Statutes of Kilkenny

In 1366, worried that the Norman settlers were becoming too Irish, the English Government introduced the Statutes of Kilkenny, a law that outlawed adopting Irish customs and ways.

Intermarrying between Norman and Irish nobility was common.

14 1459
The Pale declares itself independent

Many of the Anglo-Irish had land in the Pale, what was left of the English power base, and an area covering the counties surrounding Dublin. Unhappy with being ruled from England, a parliament was held in the Pale—and the Anglo-Irish nobility decided that Ireland should only have to follow laws that their parliament or Great Councils of Ireland decided upon.

15 **1534** Silken Thomas

Thomas Fitzgerald, or 'Silken Thomas', was born into a powerful Anglo-Irish family, the Earls of Kildare. His grandfather and his father had both clashed many times with royal authority. In 1534 Thomas led a rebellion against King Henry VIII, which was rapidly crushed by Henry's forces.

Silken Thomas (named after the silk fringes he and his men wore) spent two years in the Tower of London before being hanged.

16 **1536** Foundation of the Church of Ireland

Under Henry's rule, England had broken away from Catholicism. Henry decided that as part of his kingdom, Ireland should do the same, and so in 1536 he arranged a special parliament in Dublin which introduced a new Church of Ireland.

Almost all of the Irish, both Gaelic and Anglo-Irish, were Catholic, but the new Church was a form of Protestantism. The Catholic monasteries were disbanded and their land sold. Despite parliament's decision, most people ignored the new rules and kept their faith secretly.

The wealth of the monastery land made them a very valuable asset.

17   1541   Henry VIII declares himself King of Ireland

Henry VIII was a temperamental but formidable ruler, marrying six wives, two of whom he beheaded!

King Henry VIII was determined to enforce his authority over Ireland, so in 1541 he called another parliament proposing that he become the King of Ireland. Before this, an English king could only claim the lordship of Ireland.

As part of his plan to 'anglicise', or 'make English' the country, Henry also started the process of 'plantation'. A plantation was where land was confiscated from some troublesome Catholic landowners and given to, or 'planted by' loyal Protestant supporters of the British crown.

18   1551   Book of Common Prayer first book printed in Ireland

After Henry died, his son, the young Edward VI became King of England. One of the things that Edward did was pass a law that said the English Book of Common Prayer, an Anglican prayer book, must be read in Irish churches. As most Irish people did not speak very much or even any English, an Irish translation of the Book of Common Prayer was printed in Dublin in 1551, and became the very first book printed in Ireland.

Not using the Book of Common Prayer could result in a fine, and frequently refusing to use it could lead to life in prison!

1565 Desmond's first rebellion

Ireland was a strategically important place, mostly because of the wars going on between England, Spain, and France. To keep Ireland under English control, Queen Elizabeth I 'planted' the land in Ireland with Protestant English settlers.

Angry at the loss of land, James Fitzmaurice Fitzgerald, a devoted Catholic and opponent of Elizabeth, started the first Desmond rebellion in 1569 by attacking an English

After the first Desmond rebellion, about 700 rebels and supporters were executed and anything considered Irish was banned, including the Brehon Laws.

colony near Kerrycurihy, then Cork itself, as well as any other Irish clans who refused to help him. Thomas Butler, Earl of Ormonde, fought against him with combined forces of his own army, some Irish clans who were enemies of the Fitzgeralds, and English forces. A long period of bloodshed followed, where many of the lands around Cork were reduced to a burnt cinder.

Eventually the rebels fled to the Kerry Mountains and in 1573 surrendered, while James Fitzmaurice fled to mainland Europe.

29 1642 Battle of Benburb

During the Ulster rebellion, Scottish soldiers had come to protect the settlers, but kept running into Owen Roe O'Neill's Catholic forces. The two sides fought at Benburb, on the banks of the River Blackwater. O'Neill's well-trained forces won, and pushing the Scottish backward with pikes, trapped them by the water's edge.

Owen Roe O'Neill was a veteran commander of the Spanish Army, and the nephew of Hugh O'Neill.

30 Sept 1649 Cromwell's Siege of Drogheda

In 1649, Oliver Cromwell came to Ireland with a 12,000-strong army intending to reconquer the country for English Parliamentarians, who had just won the English Civil War.

Drogheda, a town of major tactical importance to Cromwell, was held by Irish that had not supported the Parliamentarians during the war. A note demanding surrender was delivered, but those inside refused, so the stone walls were cannoned. Cromwell ordered that 'no quarter', or 'no mercy', be shown, and the inhabitants of the town, some 3,500 people, were slaughtered.

Fleeing the massacre, a group took shelter in a church, which Cromwell's forces then burned down around them.

31 1654
To hell or to Connaught

Cromwell made a law which said that any Irish who owned land east of the Shannon must give it up and go to live on the poor soil of Connaught. Any who did not move by 1 May 1654 would be executed or sold into slavery. The phrase 'to hell or to Connaught' described the pain of the choice.

Cromwell's deputy in Ireland said of the Burren, 'It is a country where there is not enough water to drown a man, wood enough to hang one, nor earth enough to bury him.'

32 1681
Execution of Oliver Plunkett

After Cromwell's conquest, Catholicism was outlawed, but Archbishop of Armagh Oliver Plunkett was keen to bring back the Church in Ireland. He built schools for children and to train clergy. Accused by the English Government of plotting a rebellion, he was arrested, found guilty and then hung, drawn and quartered.

33 1689
The Siege of Derry

Having lost his throne, the Catholic King James II hoped Ireland might be loyal to him. Marching on Derry, the gates were shut against his army, and 15 weeks of starvation followed in the city, with 8,000 people dying.

It is said that 13 young apprentice boys shut the gates against James' oncoming army.

34   1 July 1690   The Battle of the Boyne

The Williamite War was the war fought between Catholic James II, who was fighting for the return of his crown, and Protestant William of Orange, who intended to put down James' rebellion. In Ireland, most Catholic Irish had supported James because they wanted their right to own land returned and believed James II might help. Fought on 1 July 1691 at a vital crossing point on the banks of the River Boyne, William went into battle with the biggest invading army ever seen in Ireland, a force of 36,000 with a massive amount of artillery.

James' 25,000-strong forces were much less well-equipped. William's plan was to split his forces and trap James, so he sent about a third of his army off on a diversion, drawing most of the Jacobites after them, leaving many less at the main battlefied. Outnumbered, pelted by artillery fire, James retreated. Many of the Irish infantry deserted as the Williamites advanced, and by the end of the day they were victorious. James then fled back to France and William kept the throne.

The victory of William of Orange is remembered by the Ulster Protestant community every year on the 12th of July during parades and celebrations known as 'The Twelfth'.

35) 1691 Battle of Aughrim

A high cross stands near the battleground to commemorate one of the bloodiest formal battles in Irish history.

After James fled, the Jacobite forces in Ireland fought on. In 1691, Jacobite forces met the Williamites at Aughrim, Co. Galway. Despite early success for the Jacobites, after their leader the Marquis de St Ruth was killed by a cannonball, their cavalry panicked and fled. The Williamites' superior forces easily slaughtered the remaining infantry, destroying any hopes of victory for the Jacobites.

36) 1695-1728 The Penal Laws

From 1695, harsh laws designed to limit the power and prosperity of Irish Catholics were introduced. Known as the Penal Laws, they decreed that Catholics could not sit in Parliament, work as a sheriff, lawyer, or judge, own a gun, or buy land. One law that proved to be disastrous was that land owned by a Catholic must be divided between all his sons on his death. Thus, as time passed, Catholics had smaller and smaller plots of land to live on.

As schools for Catholics were also illegal, secret 'hedge schools' were common.

(37) 1713-1726 Jonathan Swift writes *Gulliver's Travels*

Swift's other writing was very critical of the brutality of English rule in Ireland, making him an unwilling hero to the Irish.

Born in Dublin to an English father, Jonathan Swift served as a Vicar in the Church of Ireland before making his name in England as a writer and politican and being appointed the Dean of St Patrick's Cathedral in Dublin. Not very fond of the Irish or of Ireland, Swift did not enjoy his time in Dublin, but wrote the famous book, *Gulliver's Travels*, while living there.

(38) 1739-1741 Famine

Starting in December 1739, the 'Great Frost' hit Ireland like a sledgehammer. Lasting almost two years, freezing temperatures in the winter of 1739 froze solid the potatoes that were the staple diet of poor Irish Catholics. This made them inedible. Potatoes were a high-energy food that would grow on poor land. In spring 1740 a drought followed the freeze and any surviving crop failed to thrive, so vast numbers of the Irish population began to starve.

Relief schemes were created by Samuel Cooke, the Lord Mayor of Dublin, and the Archbishop of Armagh Hugh Boulter, who paid for the feeding of the poor of Dublin.

(39) 13 Apr 1742 — World premiere of Handel's Messiah in Dublin

Created in a burst of brilliance, Handel's Messiah, a piece of music famous even today, more than 270 years later, was written in only 24 days. Handel's music was often considered blasphemous, as were theatres and music halls, so it was decided that it would premiere in Dublin instead of in London, as part of a series of charity concerts in Neal's Music Hall, Fishamble Street.

Dean of St Patrick's, Jonathan Swift, had Handel's production stopped for a time, demanding that the proceeds go to charity.

(40) 1759 — Foundation of Guinness

The name 'stout' came from the phrase 'an extra stout porter', meaning an extra strong and full-bodied beer.

In 1759, Arthur Guinness took out a 9,000-year lease on a small brewery at St James' Gate, Dublin. Guinness realised that the imported beers from London that were ruining the small Irish brewing industry could be improved on, so he started to brew the dark English beer 'porter'. The beer took off, and today Guinness is the most popular alcoholic drink in Ireland, making up more than a quarter of all beer sold.

(41) 1779 First parade of Volunteers in Dublin

In 1778, Henry Grattan, leader of the Irish Parliament, secured permission to create a militia to protect the country from foreign invasion. By the end of the year 1799, there were over 40,000 Volunteers. Grattan pushed for a removal of the unfair trade laws that hurt the Irish economy, in a show of power, the Volunteers paraded through Dublin with the slogan, 'Free Trade or a Speedy Revolution' on their cannons. Alarmed, the English Government agreed.

Pushed by Grattan, in 1782 the Irish Parliament demanded freedom to make Irish laws without Britain's consent. For 20 years after, the Irish Parliament was called 'Grattan's Parliament' in his honour.

(42) 1795 Foundation of Orange Order

In the North, secret societies that maimed cattle and destroyed property sprang up. In 1795, a violent meeting of the Presbyterian Peep O' Day Boys and Catholic Defenders ended in several Catholic deaths, and the first Orange Order lodge was established later that night.

The very first Orange Order marches took place in Portadown, Lurgan, and Waringstown in 1796.

(43) 1798 Rebellion in Wexford, Antrim and Down

Inspired by the revolutionary ideas of the 1789 French Revolution, The Society of United Irishmen was formed in 1791 and led by Theobald Wolfe Tone. Its aim was the equality and freedom of all Irishmen of all religions. From the start the rebellion had bad luck – many of the Dublin leaders were arrested in the days before the uprising, leaving the rising short on organised leadership. With Dublin already defeated, on 24 May the rest of the country rebelled and was quickly crushed – except for Wexford. A band of rebels under the leadership of Fr John Murphy, a Catholic priest, stormed Enniscorthy and then Wexford before suffering devastating defeats at the next few battles and regrouping to lick their wounds at Vinegar Hill, outside Enniscorthy.

The rebellion led to atrocities on both sides, such as at Scullabogue, where over 100 suspected loyalist prisoners were burnt alive in a barn.

Meanwhile, in Ulster the United Irishmen rose in support of Wexford. After Antrim's rising was defeated, on 10 June (now called 'Pike Sunday') Co. Down rebelled. A shopkeeper called Henry Munro led the rebels into battle at Ballynahinch where the fight raged for two days before they were defeated with several hundred dead. On 16 June, Munro was hanged and decapitated outside his own front door, thus ending the Ulster rebellion.

Meanwhile, at Vinegar Hill 20,000 British soldiers surrounded the rebels. In the end the battle lasted only two hours, as the badly equipped rebels were hammered by artillery, suffering hundreds of casualties.

(44) 1798 French force lands in Mayo and Donegal

From August 1798, several small French reinforcements landed in Mayo and Donegal and had some small victories, but with no reinforcements coming from France and the rebellion crushed in the rest of the country, the French surrendered. Wolfe Tone was arrested after the ship he was on, the Hoche, surrendered and was brought to Dublin.

Tone asked to be executed like a soldier and shot. Instead, Tone was sentenced to hang and so cut his own throat while in prison.

(45) 1801 Act of Union

Though Pitt had every intention of bringing in Catholic Emancipation, King George III refused, and so, unable to make good on his promises, Pitt resigned as Prime Minister.

To ensure no more Irish rebellions, the English Prime Minister William Pitt decided that the best solution was to form a Union between the two countries. This meant that the Irish Parliament would be disbanded and Irish politicians would be represented in the Parliament in Westminster. Hinting that he would make Catholic Emancipation a priority after the Union, Pitt quickly gained the support of the Catholic population, but the Protestant Irish Parliament remained hostile. Bribery was used and in March 1800 the Irish Parliament agreed.

23 July 1803 Robert Emmet's Rising

Expelled from Trinity College in 1798 for his links with the United Irishmen, Robert Emmet hatched a plot to seize Dublin Castle in 1803. Using money from his inheritance, Emmet had manufactured new weapons for the struggle, including new varieties of explosives, but a fire at the store of these weapons alerted the authorities to the plot. The rising was a disaster, with only a handful of the 2000 Emmet had expected arriving, then rioting drunkenly through Dublin and murdering Lord Kilwarden, a local judge. After going into hiding, Emmet moved his hiding place to be near his sweetheart, Sarah Curran, and was captured. He was tried and sentenced to death, and on 20 September on Thomas Street in Dublin he was hanged, then his body beheaded.

The hanging of Robert Emmet.

47   15 Aug 1808
Foundation of the Christian Brothers

In 1802, Edmund Rice, a rich Waterford merchant, opened his first Catholic day school for poor children. The laws illegalising Catholic education were still in force and there were very few educational resources for the poor. Free and open to anyone, by 1808 there were six schools across the country and in the same year the staff, including Rice himself, took vows under the Bishop of Waterford and became a new order, the Presentation Brothers, who would later be renamed the Christian Brothers.

In the early days, at a Presentation Brothers' school the master and his assistant would have up to 150 students, all grouped not by age, but by learning ability.

48   1829
Daniel O'Connell becomes known as 'Liberator of the Nation'

Sackville Street, Dublin's main street, was renamed O'Connell Street in 1924 in honour of Daniel O'Connell. His statue now stands facing O'Connell Bridge.

Sickened by the violence of 1798, politician Daniel O'Connell believed that freedom for Ireland and for Catholics could be achieved by peaceful ends. When he won a seat in the British Parliament but could not take it due to being Catholic, the Government realised that if they did not give in there would be yet another rebellion. Thus, in 1829 the Catholic Relief Act was passed and the Catholic Irish gave O'Connell his famous name, 'The Liberator'.

49

1 Sept 1831
Dublin Zoo opens

On 1 September 1831, Dublin Zoological Gardens first opened its doors. The Zoological Society of Ireland, founded a year before, was given a five-acre portion of land inside Phoenix Park by the Lord Lieutenant of Ireland to build a zoo along the same lines as the one that was so much admired in London. London Zoo donated all of the animals first on display. Now the zoo has expanded to 59 acres and is involved in conservation and research in partnership with other zoos all over the world.

The most visitors to the zoo in one day was 20,000 people in 1838, who came for an open day celebrating Queen Victoria's coronation.

1845-1846 The Great Famine

An Gorta Mór, or 'The Great Hunger', was one of the darkest periods in Irish history. Because of the Penal Laws, any land a Catholic left in his will had to be divided between his sons, so now vast numbers of families farmed tiny plots of land. In this tight space, the nourishing potato was grown almost exclusively, and before the famine one-third of the population of eight million survived on this one crop. In 1845, a fungus-like disease called the potato blight ruined more than one-third of the crop across Ireland, infecting the plants from below. Although the plants looked healthy from above ground, the potatoes were rotten when harvested. In 1846, the disease had spread to the whole country, leaving millions starving – but hopes were pinned on the next year's crop. The despair when this year's harvest was found to be infected can only be imagined. Without anything else to live on or any crop to sell to pay rent, starving peasants were evicted from holdings by landlords. Hundreds of thousands of people died of disease and hunger or emigrated on 'coffin ships'. In his last speech to parliament, Daniel O'Connell said: 'I predict that one-quarter of the population will perish unless you come to Ireland's relief'.

O'Connell's prediction was not far wrong – over a million died of starvation and diseases such as cholera. About a million and a half emigrated to Britain and the New World. Thousands made the long six-week journey across the Atlantic in crowded, filthy ships.

51 11 Sept 1855 Ireland's first ever cricket international

Cricket has a long history in Ireland – believed to have been first introduced by the British military and then brought home by boys educated in Britain. Though it was likely played many years earlier, the first recorded game took place in 1792 in Phoenix Park. In 1855, in Ireland's first ever cricket international, the Irish national team beat the Gentlemen of England in Dublin by 107 runs.

52 1858 Irish Republican Brotherhood formed

James Stephens was brought up in Kilkenny.

Unlike Daniel O'Connell, Irish revolutionary sympathiser James Stephens was dedicated to overthrowing British rule in Ireland by whatever means necessary and felt that O'Connell's peaceful methods would never result in political freedom. Formed in 1858, the IRB believed that Ireland had a natural right to govern itself.

Charles Stewart Parnel was a cricket fan as a young man and played for the Dublin Phoenix team for a while – but in 1866, a committee meeting complained that he had not paid his subscription!

53   29 March 1859   First copy of the *Irish Times* printed

The first edition of the *Irish Times* was published on 29 March 1859 at No. 4 Lower Abbey Street in Dublin. Founded by Major Lawrence Knox, it was originally the mouthpiece of moderate Protestant nationalists. In 1974, a Trust was formed to ensure that the *Irish Times* remained an independent newspaper, free from any form of control by groups interested in putting forward hidden agendas.

The Trust is the only one of its kind in Ireland and is one of very few newspapers worldwide to have such protection.

54   1867   Rise of Fenians and the Manchester Martyrs

The Fenians, as members of the IRB were now called, rebelled in 1867, but suffered from disorganisation and were quickly defeated. In England, a group of Fenians attacked a horse-drawn police van taking two captured Fenian leaders to jail and, while shooting off the lock, killed a police officer inside with the keys.

Michael Larkin, William Philip Allen, and Michael O'Brien, were publicly hanged at Salford Gaol and afterwards became known as the Manchester Martyrs.

(55) 1870 The Home Rule Association set up by Isaac Butt

In May 1870, Isaac Butt founded the Home Government Association with the hope of bringing in self-government of some kind for Ireland. A Protestant educated at Trinity College, Butt felt that since O'Connell's time 30 years before, Home Rule had been pushed for by the Irish, and now that the Fenians were active, the time had come to make it happen – while keeping some protection for the Protestant minority.

Butt wanted an Irish Parliament separate from the Westminster Parliament, but not complete independence from Britain.

(56) 1872 First Dublin trams put into service

Dublin's first ever tram system, a horse-drawn tram travelling to Terenure, opened in 1872. The trams were incredibly popular, allowing the ordinary people who could not afford to buy or rent a carriage to get around the city easily. By 1896, the first electric trams were running to and from Dalkey, and four years later the whole system was fully electric.

Some trams were open-top and some covered to keep the rain off.

57 · 21 Oct 1879 · The Irish National Land League founded

Anglo-Irish landowner and nationalist politician Charles Stewart Parnell combined the 'land campaign' with the idea of Home Rule. In 1879, in Castlebar, Co. Mayo, Parnell became the president of the Land League, which aimed to secure more rights for small tenant farmers. The Land League's methods of getting what they wanted were peaceful – Parnell ordered a boycott of anyone who moved into a farm where the previous farmer had been evicted, and also of landlords who charged rack rents and evicted tenants.

58 · 1881 · Land Act

The struggle between peasants and landlords, led by Parnell and the Land League, became known as the 'Land War', which pursued the 'Three Fs' of fair rent, fixture of tenancy, and freedom to sell. Finally, in 1881 parliament was forced to pass the Land Act, which made fair rates of rent law.

A famous public speaker, Parnell said, 'No man has the right to fix the boundary of a nation'.

Parnell was in love with Kitty O'Shea, the wife of an Irish MP. When in 1899 O'Shea asked for a divorce, Parnell's reputation collapsed and many abandoned him.

(59) 1 Nov 1884 Gaelic Athletic formed by Michael Cusack

In 1884, Michael Cusack, a teacher and founder of the Civil Service Academy which trained students for civil service and other professional exams, set up the Gaelic Athletic Association (GAA).

A keen sportsman, Cusack was also passionately interested in Gaelic culture and became involved in the Gaelic revival movement, which was the promotion of interest in Irish Gaelic culture, including the Gaelic

The first All-Ireland Final was played in March 1896 at what is now Croke Park. Tipperary beat Kilkenny in the All-Ireland Hurling Final.

language, folklore, music and so on, with the aim of strengthening an Irish national identity. Cusack founded the GAA to promote traditional Irish sports such as hurling, handball and Gaelic football, while making sport available to all social classes and establishing clubs that would organise matches across the counties of Ireland.

With links to the IRB and the Fenians, who reportedly often recruited from the ranks of GAA members, and Michael Cusack at its helm, the GAA had strong nationalist ties. In fact, from 1902 to 1971 'Rule 27' banned GAA members from playing, watching, or furthering the cause of non-Gaelic games. This included soccer, rugby, hockey and cricket, and breaking Rule 27 resulted in expulsion from the GAA. In 1913, the GAA purchased a plot of land for £3,500 and named it Croke Park in honour of Archbishop Thomas Croke, the first patron of the GAA.

(60) July 1893 — Gaelic League founded by Douglas Hyde

In 1893, The Gaelic League was founded by Eoin MacNeill and Douglas Hyde to promote the Irish language, and to encourage Irish culture through activities such as Irish dancing, music, and poetry. By 1904 the League had 593 branches and 50,000 members. Though not a political group, it attracted many nationalists, and many later political leaders and rebels first met there.

The Gaelic League had an interest in all things Gaelic – note the Gaelic-style knot work of the early logo.

(61) 14 Feb 1895 — First performance of *The Importance of Being Earnest*

Wilde also wrote the beautiful children's stories 'The Selfish Giant' and 'The Happy Prince', where the Prince gives everything he has to the poor and the needy.

On St Valentine's Day in 1895, *The Importance of Being Earnest* first opened at the St James' Theatre in London. A dramatist, writer, scholar, and public wit, Oscar Wilde was born in Dublin to intellectual parents and was an outstanding student at Trinity College and later Oxford. At the height of his fame when the play opened, today his plays and fiction are still considered some of the finest in the English language.

(62) 1897
Bram Stoker's *Dracula* published

Born in Dublin in 1847, Bram Stoker was the son of a civil servant and followed in his father's footsteps before moving to London to become manager of a theatre. *Dracula* was published in 1897, and though it did not cause much of a sensation at the time, over the next century it became one of the world's most famous stories, with over 100 Dracula films now having been made.

(63) 1905
Sinn Féin founded

Sinn Féin was founded in 1905 by United Irishman newspaper editor Arthur Griffith. The name Sinn Féin means 'We Ourselves' in Irish.

Starting as an Irish cultural group, Sinn Féin gradually became a nationalist political party. Wishing to create a separate Irish Republic, it wanted Irish politicians to leave the English Parliament and establish an Irish alternative.

(64) 20 Dec 1909
The Volta, Ireland's first cinema, opens

On Monday, 20 December 1909, Ireland's very first picture house, the Volta Cinema, opened its doors. Living in the bustling Italian city of Trieste where cinema was becoming popular, the Dublin-born writer James Joyce had the idea to bring cinema to Ireland. With money from his Italian friends, Joyce set up the Volta Electric Theatre on Mary Street.

The Volta has 420 seats and was renamed the Lyceum in 1921. It closed in 1948.

PICTURE VOLTA THEATRE

(69) April 1916 Easter Rising

The Easter Rebellion started at the General Post Office (GPO) in Dublin on Easter Monday, 24 April 1916. A loose group of organisations planned the rebellion, including the secret Irish Republican Brotherhood (IRB) and the Irish Citizen Army. The central group were members of the secretive militant organisation, the IRB, led by Patrick Pearse, a poet and teacher. He read out a document on the steps of the GPO proclaiming the existence of an Irish Republic and a new temporary government.

Many Irish people had felt for a long time that they were second-class citizens in the British empire and wanted Irish independence. They were unhappy that Britain had stopped plans for Irish home rule in 1914. The rebels occupied the GPO and other large Dublin buildings and attacked British forces. The British Army fought back until, by 29 April, the rebels only occupied the GPO. By the time they surrendered, about 300 people had been killed and 1,000 wounded. The rebellion had little public support, as Dubliners were confused at what was happening and angry at the destruction of their city. But the decision of the British to execute the 15 leaders of the Rising by firing squad and destroy their bodies caused a lot of anger, turning the opinion of the Irish public against the British and celebrating the rebels as heroes.

The sacrifice made by the leaders of the 1916 Rising were commemorated by the great Irish poet W.B. Yeats in the poem Easter 1916.

(70) 1919 Irish Volunteers and Citizen Army merge to form IRA

After the Rising, the Irish Volunteers tried to reorganise themselves after the fighting, and a convention in Dublin in autumn 1917 was headed by Eamon de Valera, the new president of Sinn Féin.

When Ireland was later delcared an independent Republic, the Irish Volunteers were joined by many members of the Irish Citizen Army and declared themselves the army of the new, illegal, Republic – the 'Irish Republican Army'.

(71) 1919 The first Dáil meets

In the British general election of 1918, Sinn Féin won 70% of the Irish seats and declared itself to be the Dáil Éireann, the Irish Parliament. Though allowed to sit in the British Parliament, they refused, called the first Dáil on 21 January, and introduced the Declaration of Independance.

The Dáil today. Dáil Éireann means 'Assembly of Ireland' in Irish.

(72) 1919 War of Independence

Black and Tans were sent in to fight the IRA. Undisciplined and violent, after an IRA murder they would often take revenge on civilians.

On the day of the first Dáil, two Royal Irish Constables were murdered, sparking the the War of Independence. Bands of IRA members under the command of Michael Collins killed, in secret, individual police officers, members of the British Army and people who worked for the Government.

73 1920
Act for partition of Ireland passed

At the height of the War of Independence, hoping to end the ongoing violence, the British Government passed the Government of Ireland Act.

Ireland was split into Northern and Southern Ireland, each with its own parliament under control of the parliament in London.

BELFAST

DUBLIN

74 1921
Anglo-Irish Treaty signed

The British Prime Minister David Lloyd George negotiated a truce between the IRA and the British on 11 July 1921, ending the war, and after four months of talks with a team headed by Michael Collins and Arthur Griffith, the Anglo-Irish Treaty was signed by Collins on behalf of the IRA. The Dáil voted 64–57 to accept, giving Southern Ireland full control of their own affairs – but with King George V as the Head of State.

Collins wrote of the Treaty, 'Will anyone be satisfied? I tell you this: I signed my death warrant'.

75 22 Aug 1922
Michael Collins dies

Collins knew that many would consider signing the treaty a betrayal, but did what he believed had to be done. The IRA split, with Collins' pro-treaty side fighting against those who did not support it, and a bitter, violent Civil War lasted from 1922 to 1923. Collins was shot in an ambush at Béal na mBláth, Co. Cork, in August 1922, signalling the end of the war.

76 · 1922
Irish Free State established

On 6 December, during the Civil War, the Irish Free State was established. Ireland became self-governed, but remained a 'dominion' or state of the British Empire. After Michael Collins and Arthur Griffiths died in the war, the leadership of the Free State went to William Cosgrave, veteran of the 1916 Easter Rising.

77 · April 1923
Sean O'Casey's first play opens

First performed in the Abbey Theatre in 1923, *The Shadow of a Gunman* was set only a few years before, during the War of Independence. The audience thought the play disrespectful, and also disliked O'Casey's later plays, which were critical of the violent cost of the struggle on the poor.

In 1926, the Abbey audience started a riot at O'Casey's play *The Plough and the Stars!*

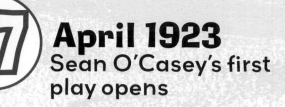

78 · 14 Nov 1923
WB Yeats wins the Nobel Literature Prize

Yeats wrote famous plays and poems, and was a member of the Irish Senate for many years.

Poet WB Yeats hated the violent Nationalism that had silenced the Protestant minority after the struggle for independence. Awarded the Nobel Prize for Literature in 1923, Yeats is one of Ireland's finest writers.

79

1932 Eamon de Valera in power

De Valera quickly removed the Oath of Allegience to the British Crown that politicians had to swear before taking their seats in parliament.

De Valera, still considered a hero by the public, created his own party called Fianna Fail in 1926, and in 1932 stormed to victory in the Irish general election. Over the next few years, de Valera concentrated on making Ireland more self-sufficient.

80

20 May 1932 Amelia Earhart lands at Culmore, Co. Derry

Amelia Earhart was the first woman to fly solo across the Atlantic. In 1932, she set off from Newfoundland in Canada to fly to Paris, but instead came down in a farmer's field in Ballyarnott, Co. Derry. The first person to reach the little red plane, a farm-hand, asked Earhart where she'd come from. She replied, 'America!'

Earhart's flight took 15 hours in her Lockheed Vega 5b.

81

1937 Constitution of Ireland

Taking two years and a team of De Valera's men to create it, in 1937 the Constitution of Ireland was voted in. It brought some changes: Ireland was now a totally independent country, and instead of a Prime Minister Ireland had a 'Taoiseach', meaning 'chieftain' or 'king'. Under the new Constitution, Ireland also got a new name, changing from 'The Irish Free State' to 'Éire', the Irish for 'Ireland'.

82 **1939** Outbreak of World War II – the Emergency

Ireland was now totally independent of Britain, so when World War II broke out in 1939 Ireland remained neutral. Taoiseach de Valera had based his whole political career on total separation, and fearing another bloody civil war if Ireland supported Britain and introduced conscription into the British Army (where citizens of a country may be called to fight in a war), de Valera's government declared a state of emergency. Though Ireland was neutral, it bent the rules, not discouraging the 50,000 Irishmen who fought in the war from joining the British Army. It gave aid to Allied-force planes and boats, while Axis forces were detained after if they were rescued and captured. Due to its neutrality, Éire did not suffer deliberate air bombings like England, though food rationing was common.

Northern Ireland, however, was at war. Airfields were built, the shipyards supported the Allies with supplies, and on 15 April 1941, the Belfast Blitz saw 200 German bombers destroy 56,000 homes and kill around 1,000 people in air raids, leaving a shattered city, where 100,000 out of a population of 450,000 were left homeless.

By 4 a.m. the whole city appeared to be ablaze and a telegram asking for aid was sent to de Valera in the south of Ireland.

Help was sent and for three days in Belfast the battle against the fires raged.

The Good Friday Agreement, or Belfast Agreement, was a major turning point in the move towards peace in Northern Ireland. On Good Friday, 10 April 1998, the agreement was signed by the United Kingdom and Republic of Ireland. It meant that instead of the old system of government, the North would move towards a government that included all groups, unionist and nationalist, with a structure in place to make sure that the two opposing camps could not vote against each other. It was such a step forward in Northern Ireland because it had never had a government that both Nationalists and Unionists would work together within.

Before the agreement was reached, Northern Ireland voted on it, with a massive 71% saying yes. In the Republic, the vote was whether to change the Constitution to support the agreement, which meant giving up any claim to the six counties of Northern Ireland. 94% voted yes. The assembly got off to a shaky start – Unionists refused to participate alongside Sinn Féin until they were sure that the IRA had given up its weapons and stopped meeting. However, the agreement was the very first of its kind ever possible in war-torn Northern Ireland, and also included a reducing of British Army troops on the streets, and a commitment from both paramilitary sides to give up their weapons.

THE AGREEMENT
It's your decision

There have been many problems along the way, but the commitment to a peaceful way of solving conflict gives many people hope of permanent peace.

(96) 15 Aug 1998
Omagh bombing

In 1998, the Real IRA set off a bomb that killed 29 innocent people in the busy town of Omagh. Unhappy with Sinn Féin's strategy of pursuing peace, they had sent a warning by phone, but the bomb had been placed in a different area of town. 500 lbs of explosives went off right where the inhabitants had been evacuated to, killing 21.

This was the most shocking terrorist incident in modern Northern Irish history, with a woman pregnant with twins killed, as well as six children and hundreds wounded.

(97) 2002
Currency changes from punt to euro

On 1 January 1999, the euro became the single currency of 17 of the 27 EU member countries. In Ireland, though the euro was introduced in 1999, it wasn't until 2002 that the Irish punt stopped being used.

You can tell which country a euro coin is from by the back. An Irish euro coin is engraved with a harp.

(98) Dec 2004
Robbery of Belfast's Northern Bank

On 19 December, three masked men forced their way into the house of Northern Bank official Chris Ward and held him and his family hostage. Ward's supervisor Kevin McMullan had also been held hostage, and the next day both were forced to go to work and allow £26.5 million to be loaded into a van in crates. It is one of the largest robberies in UK history.

(99) 2007 New Northern Ireland Assembly meets for the first time

Gerry Adams and Ian Paisley, longtime political enemies and leaders of Republican Sinn Féin and Unionist DUP, agreed to share a government – a turning point in Irish history.

From 2002, the Northern Ireland Assembly had been suspended because of disagreements between the parties and people began to worry it might fail. When it started up again in 2007, after the new, politically neutral Police Service of Northern Ireland was given support by Sinn Féin, and the DUP agreed to support sharing power in the government with republicans and nationalists, there was great relief.

(100) 2009 Ireland's rugby team wins the Grand Slam and Triple Crown in the Six Nations

Ten years after the Five Nations tournament became the Six Nations tournament, the Irish rugby team won the championship. Led by Brian O'Driscoll, this was to be their first win since 1985. They were able to win the Triple Crown and their second ever Grand Slam.

The Irish team's winning of the Grand Slam was even more impressive as they played more away games than home games.